# HELLO KITTY'S GUIDE TO EVERYTHING NICE

by Julia Marsden

Do's, Don'ts, Manners, and Mistakes

SCHOLASTIC INC.

New York     Toronto     London     Auckland     Sydney
Mexico City     New Delhi     Hong Kong     Buenos Aires

Book design by Kay Petronio

12 11 10 9 8 7 6 5 4 3 2          5 6 7 8 9/0

Printed in the U.S.A.

First printing, September 2004

# Table of Contents

# PART 1

# Why Manners Matter

## Hello Kitty Explains It All

Have you ever wondered about the "right" way to introduce a friend to your parents, how to plan a perfect party, or what foods you can eat with your fingers? Wonder no more! Hello Kitty is here to clue you in. These pages are packed with info about how to be perfectly polite. Hello Kitty knows that good manners are more than just do's and don'ts. They're a way of making the world a nicer place in which to live.

HELLO KITTY SAYS: "Treat others as you would like to be treated."

## Hello Kitty's Top Reasons Why Manners Matter

* Good manners put people at ease.

* Good manners impress people.

* Good manners build self-esteem.

* Good manners are attractive.

* Good manners allow you to get along better with people.

* Good manners make you appear more confident, which makes you feel more confident.

* Good manners make others feel good about themselves.

good manners!

## Words That Work Wonders

Hello Kitty knows that little words and phrases like *Please*, *Thank you*, *May I*, *You're welcome*, *Excuse me*, and *I'm sorry* have a big impact when it comes to getting along with others. Here's her advice on how to use them.

| DO SAY | WHEN | DON'T SAY |
|---|---|---|
| "Please." | You want something. | "Give me that." |
| "Thank you." | You receive something— a gift, a compliment, a loan, a favor, service in a restaurant or at a store—or when someone does something for you. | "This is strange." <br><br> "I already have one of these." <br><br> "Hmmm." |
| "You're welcome." | Someone says, "Thank you." | "Huh? Oh, sure. Whatever." |
| "May I . . ." | You want permission to do something. | "Let me . . ." |
| "Excuse me." | You yawn, move through a crowd, cut or pass in front of someone, or you must interrupt. | "Boy, am I tired." <br><br> "Watch out!" <br><br> "Hey!" |
| "Excuse me?" | You don't understand something someone has said. | "Huh?" <br> "What?" <br> "I don't get it!" |
| "I'm sorry." | You're late, you bump into someone, or you break or spill something. | Nothing |

# First Impressions

## The Importance of Introductions

### Ask Hello Kitty

**Q:** Hello Kitty, what should I do when I'm being introduced to someone?

**A:** Hold your head high. Look the person you're being introduced to in the eye and shake his/her hand. Then, using a strong and confident voice, say "Hello," "How are you?" or "It's nice to meet you."

Hello Kitty knows that at school or parties, or when others have neglected to introduce you, it's perfectly polite to introduce yourself.

"Hi, I'm Hello Kitty. I'm Tracy's friend."

When it comes to making introductions, Hello Kitty says:

*An older person should be introduced before a younger person.*

"Mama, I'd like you to meet my friend Fifi."

*A female should be introduced before a male.*

"Miss Smith, this is my father, Mr. White."

*A dignitary (elected official, religious leader) should be introduced first.*

"Mayor, may I introduce you to my sister, Mimmy."

# Hello Kitty's Helpful Hints

DO stand when you're being introduced to someone.

DON'T be afraid to be the first one to put your hand forward to shake hands.

DO use a person's title if they have one. "It's nice to meet you, Dr. Jones."

DON'T worry if you forget the name of the person you are introducing. Just say, "I'm so sorry, but I've forgotten your name."

DO speak up if you didn't catch the name of a person you've been introduced to. Just say "I'm sorry. I didn't hear your name."

# Conversation Starters

Hello Kitty is always ready with these conversation starters. They will definitely keep the comments coming!

✺ What's your favorite movie?

✺ What good books have you read?

✺ What foods do you like the best?

✺ What's your favorite sport?

✺ What are your favorite hobbies?

# conversational courtesies

☀ Ask leading questions to show your interest in others
and to learn more about them. For example: "What do you do
in your spare time?"

☀ When another person is talking don't just say "Uh-huh, uh-huh"
and hope he or she stops talking soon so you can say something.
Give that person your full attention.

☀ Active listening involves looking at the other person,
asking questions, and responding to what's been said.

## Ask Hello Kitty

**Q:** Hello Kitty, how can I politely end a conversation?

**A:** First, it's not polite to end a conversation while someone is talking. I always wait for the other person to finish what she's saying. Then I smile and say one of the following lines:

"I've got to be going. It's been so nice talking to you."

or

"I hope to see you again soon."

or

"Take care. See you later."

# PART 3

# Family Matters

## House Rules

Hello Kitty knows that the secret to a happy family is making sure everybody does their fair share of chores. Here's a list of little things Hello Kitty does around the house. They make a big difference when it comes to sharing space with her family.

Hello Kitty always:

* makes her bed when she gets up in the morning.

* carries her plate from the table to the dishwasher or sink after meals.

* hangs up wet towels right away.

* puts her dirty clothes in a hamper.

* puts away her coat and backpack when she comes home.

☀ greets a parent who returns home.

☀ expresses appreciation for meals.
(Hello Kitty is also quick to compliment her sister, Mimmy, when she bakes her delicious cookies!)

☀ feeds the family's pets.

☀ picks up her things and puts them away.

☀ puts the TV remote and cordless phone back where they belong when she's done using them.

Hello Kitty wants to hear from you! Can you list three things that you do in your home to make sure that everyone is happy?

## TV Guidelines

Hello Kitty has a few favorite TV shows. But she always remembers her manners when it comes to television and video viewing. When a friend arrives for a visit, she turns off the TV. If her parents have company and Hello Kitty is watching a favorite show, she stops watching it long enough to say hello. Then she returns to watching her show, lowering the volume if it is too loud.

Whether Hello Kitty is enjoying a TV show or she's at the movies with friends or her family, she follows these rules: No talking, don't ask too many questions, and don't tell what's going to happen next.

no talking!

# Bathroom Behavior

After Hello Kitty has used the bathroom, she:

* rinses the sink.

* wipes the counter with a tissue or washcloth.

* gathers her toiletries and puts them away on a shelf or in a cabinet.

* uses the bathroom only for the essentials. Then she returns to her room to get dressed.

*consideration!*

## Ask Hello Kitty

**Q:** Hello Kitty, I have to share a room with my sister. How can we make the best of the situation?

**A:** I share a room with my sister, Mimmy. Our secret to making it work is being considerate of each other. Also, if we disagree, we brainstorm solutions. Make the best of the situation and enjoy having a live-in best friend!

HELLO KITTY SAYS:
"Home is where the heart is."

share

**PART 4**

# School Rules

## Be a class Act

Hello Kitty is a good student in every way! She always makes sure to practice classroom courtesy. Here are some of her simple rules:

She:

☀ listens to her teachers.

☀ doesn't speak before thinking.

☀ cleans up after herself.

☀ doesn't come to class unprepared.

☀ raises her hand before speaking.

☀ doesn't forget to be respectful of others' ideas.

☀ compliments her classmates on good work.

☀ doesn't forget to say "Please," "Thank you," "Excuse me," and "I'm sorry."

☀ keeps her hands and feet to herself.

☀ works hard in class.

☀ remembers that teachers have feelings, too.

# The Sporting Life

Spectator and Player Etiquette

Hello Kitty knows how to score points as a good team player.
Here are some rules to help you get on the winning side of
teammates, coaches, and parents.

- ☀ Learn the rules of the game.

- ☀ Control your temper.

- ☀ Respect everyone.

- ☀ Refuse to place blame on others.

- ☀ Learn from your mistakes.

- ☀ Play an honest game.

- ☀ Don't let your team down. Go to practice, keep your uniform
  clean, help out at fund-raisers, and let the coach know if you're
  going to miss a practice.

* Always show respect while the national anthem is played.

* Respect the referees.

* Shake hands with the members of the other team—no matter who wins.

## Ask Hello Kitty

**Q:** Hello Kitty, one of my teammates can be a real sore loser. Any advice?

**A:** While nobody likes to lose, learning to be graceful when a game doesn't go your way shows true sportsmanship. Remind your teammate that it's good manners to congratulate the winning players, just like she would want to be congratulated the next time her team wins!

# The Friendship Formula

## Are you a first-rate friend?

Hello Kitty put together this short quiz for you. Answer these ten questions to learn if you're a first-rate friend, or if your pal skills need improvement.

1. Are you happy when something good happens to your friend?

2. Do you give your friend a break when she's in a bad mood, knowing that everyone can have a bad day?

3. Do you introduce others to your friend?

4. Do you listen to your friend talk without changing the subject to something about you?

5. Do you sometimes let your friend choose what to do?

6. Does your friend know the true you?

7. Do you feel sad when something bad happens to your friend?

8. Do you let your friend know how special she is to you?

9. Do you forgive your friend when she's done something that has hurt you?

10. Do you recognize your friend's unique gifts and strengths?

If you answered yes to nine or more questions, congratulations! You are a first-rate pal. You know that to have good friends, you have to be a good friend. Spread the word!

If you answered yes to between six and eight questions, you're off to a good start. Reread the questions you answered no to. What could you do to change those answers to yes? Remember, friendship is a two-way street.

If you answered yes to five or fewer questions, it's time to brush up on your friendship skills. You may really appreciate your friends, but you need to practice showing it. The next time you're in a tricky friend situation, think about how you would want your friend to act toward you.

## Taking Sides

If you have more than one friend (and chances are you do!), there probably have been times when two of your friends haven't been getting along and each wants you to take her side.

Hello Kitty knows that it is not fun to be in the middle of two friends who disagree. Listen in and hear how she graciously handled this sticky situation:

"Fifi, I'm sorry that you and Rory aren't getting along right now. I know it must be upsetting to you. But I like you both too much to get caught in the middle or choose sides. Why don't you sit down and talk about the problem? I'm sure you'll solve it and get back on track."

## Telling Secrets

Keeping secrets can be difficult. Hello Kitty knows one way to be sure her secrets aren't shared: not telling secrets in the first place. But if Hello Kitty must tell someone a special secret, she makes sure to confide in one of her closest friends.

## Ask Hello Kitty

**Q:** Hello Kitty, my friend borrowed one of my favorite CDs a month ago. I really want it back. What should I do?

**A:** Sometimes being direct is the best way to get results. Simply say, "Would you please bring my CD to school? I'd like to have it back." She may have forgotten that she borrowed it. Reminding her that she has it may be all it takes to get it back.

# PART 6

# Social Calendar Clues

## How to Plan a Perfect Party

Are you thinking of throwing a bash? Hello Kitty knows that the secret to a perfect party is in the planning. If you're thinking of having a party, ask yourself these seven questions:

1. What kind of party do I want to have? (Birthday, surprise, sleepover, costume)

2. Where will the party be held? (Basement, living room, backyard, park)

3. How many people will I invite?

4. Who will I invite?

5. When will the party be held? (Weekend, evening, daytime, holiday)

6. What refreshments and snacks will be served?

7. How will I decorate?

Now you're thinking! Hello Kitty is sure that you're ready to plan a fabulous party that your friends will remember for a long time to come.

Chances are you won't be able to invite everyone you'd like to have at your party. How can you make sure that friends who are not invited don't have hurt feelings? Here are some ideas from Hello Kitty!

* Do mail or deliver invitations to friends at their homes.

* Don't hand them out at school in front of people who aren't invited.

**Q:** Hello Kitty, my mom said I could only invite three people to my birthday party. One of my friends who wasn't invited found out about the party and her feelings are hurt. What should I do?

**A:** Explain to your friend that your mom put a limit on how many people you could invite. Then consider inviting the friend to your house for an after-school get-together or a sleepover. Feeling left out isn't fun. But if your friend understands that you had a limit on how many people you could invite, she's likely to feel better.

## Sleepover Secrets

How does Hello Kitty prepare for staying overnight at a friend's house? She:

☀ packs her pajamas, toothbrush, and a sleeping bag.

* follows her friend's lead when it comes to family rules and routines.

* keeps the space she's staying in orderly and clean.

* gets permission before using the phone.

* avoids overstaying her welcome.

* brings a game to play.

* arrives with a gift for the host, like a batch of her famous Hello Kitty Crunch.

## Hello Kitty Crunch

crunch!

What you need:
* 5 cups toasted oat cereal
* 2 cups roasted almonds
* 16 oz. chocolate-covered candies

What you need to do:
Mix all the ingredients in a large bowl. Then place in a serving dish or storage container. Make sure to share your Hello Kitty Crunch with friends. It's delicious!

## Gifts Galore

*When you receive a gift,* thank the person who gave it to you. Try to say something positive, like "This is so cute!" "Wow, it's really pretty," or "This is my favorite color." Then follow up by writing a friendly thank-you note.

*When you give a gift,* wrap it in pretty paper and add a ribbon. Then tape a card on the gift with your name and the name of the recipient. Use the stickers in this book to create a handmade card for a personalized touch!

Here's a fun idea for a friendship flowerpot. Hello Kitty enjoys making this craft for her friends.

To make a friendship flowerpot, you'll need:

* white paper
* two clear plastic cups of the same size
* clear tape
* a pencil
* scissors
* stickers from this book
* colored markers
* masking tape
* ribbon
* white glue

Here's what you need to do:

1. Wrap the piece of white paper around the outside of one of the cups. Hold it in place with a small piece of tape.

2. Use a pencil to mark the paper where the top and bottom of the cup are positioned.

3. Remove the piece of tape. Then use scissors to trim the excess paper above and below the cup. Now you should have a piece of paper that fits neatly inside the cup.

4. Place the paper flat on a table and decorate it using stickers and colored markers.

5. Put the decorated paper back inside the cup. Then insert the other cup inside the first cup. Now the paper is between two cups.

6. Tape the rims of both cups with masking tape to seal out any moisture from the plant.

HELLO KITTY SAYS: "Give the gift of friendship."

7. Cover the masking tape with glue. Then decorate it with ribbons.

8. Finally, place a prepotted plant inside the decorated planter. Or you can add potting soil and seeds and watch your plant grow!

friendship

**Q:** Hello Kitty, my friend gave me a gift for the holidays, but I didn't have one for her!

**A:** If you're given a gift and don't have a present to give in return, it's extra important to let your friend know how much you appreciate her thoughtfulness. Then follow up with a thank-you note. Being especially appreciative will show the giver that you are grateful for her gift.

# PART 7

# Food for Thought

## Table Manners

### Hello Kitty's Top Ten Guide to Mealtime Manners

1. Wash your hands before sitting at the table.

2. Place your hands in your lap once you are seated.

3. Put your napkin in your lap.

4. Begin eating after everyone has been served.

5. Pass serving dishes to the right.

6. Chew with your mouth closed.

7. At the end of the meal, thank the host.

8. Place your napkin loosely on the table near your plate when you are through with your meal.

9. Push your chair under the table when you get up from the table.

10. After the meal, offer to help clean up.

## Dining Dilemmas

* *Oops!* You've knocked over your glass of water. Say "I'm sorry!" and help clean up the spill.

* *Clink!* Your fork just landed on the floor.
If you're at a friend's house, pick up the utensil and say, "Excuse me, I dropped my fork." The host will get you a new fork.
If you're at a restaurant, leave the fork on the floor. Then ask the server for a new one.

* *Uh-oh!* You took a bite of food and realize there's gristle or a seed or something strange in what you're chewing. Discreetly lift your napkin up to your mouth and remove the object from your mouth. Then place your napkin to the side of your plate.

* *Nuts!* The host appears with a small bowl of almonds and cashews. You're allergic to them. Say, "No, thank you. I'm

allergic to nuts." Then make a point of selecting something from the other foods available.

## A Perfect Setting

Hello Kitty and her sister, Mimmy, take turns setting the table before meals. At first, setting out all that silverware seemed confusing. But with practice, they've learned the basics. Now they'll teach you how to create a perfect setting.

left      HELLO KITTY      right

✳ Set each place at the table with three utensils: a knife, a fork, and a spoon. The fork is placed directly to the left of the plate. Then lay the knife directly to the right of the plate, with its cutting edge facing the plate. Finally, place the spoon directly to the right of the knife.

✳ Sometimes there are other utensils, such as a salad fork or a soupspoon. The salad fork is placed to the left of the regular fork. The soupspoon should be placed to the right of the regular spoon.

✳ Here's a rule worth remembering: The utensil farthest away from the plate is used first. Since soup and salad are eaten before the main course, eat them with the spoon and fork farthest away from your plate.

## Finger Foods

Appetizers can be plucked off the platter with your fingers or by using a toothpick, if they're provided. Sometimes there is a plate or bowl near the appetizers for used toothpicks, shells, pits, or papers that were part of the appetizer. If not, just keep them on your plate or in your napkin.

Some foods are too awkward to eat using utensils. The simple solution? Use your fingers! Here's a list of foods that are a-okay to eat with your fingers. Bon appétit!

Bon Appétit!

| | | |
|---|---|---|
| Corn on the cob | Olives | artichokes |
| French fries | Pizza | Steamed |
| Grapes | Sandwiches | asparagus |
| Hamburgers | Spareribs | Tacos |
| Hot dogs | Steamed | Tortillas |

**Q:** Hello Kitty, how do I deal with a food I don't like?

**A:** Nobody likes everything! If you're offered food you don't like, say "No, thank you." If something has already been put on your plate that you don't care for, just leave it on your plate.

# The Write Stuff

## How Inviting!

Hello Kitty loves to host parties. So she knows how important it is to create an inviting invitation. Follow her pointers for letting your friends know about your fun fiestas! Every party invitation should include the following information:

What sort of party you are hosting

Who is hosting the party

When and where the party will be held

Reply information: Some invitations include R.S.V.P., which stands for *Répondez, s'il vous plaît* (which means "reply, please" in French). If you receive an invitation with an R.S.V.P., let the host know as soon as possible if you'll attend.

Send your invitation at least two weeks before the event. Don't forget to include all the important info for your guests!

*If you're able to attend an event,* it's best to respond within a week of receiving the invitation. You should respond in the same way you received the invitation. If a friend calls on the phone to ask you to a birthday party, you can accept right on the spot or call back later with a response. A written invitation with an R.S.V.P. and a phone number should be accepted or declined by telephone by the date indicated on the invitation.

*If you're unable to attend an event,* express your regrets by thanking the person for the invitation. Then give a short explanation such as: "Thank you for inviting me, but my family has plans for that day" or "I'm sorry, but I'm not able to come."

R.S.V.P.

Here's an invitation that Hello Kitty recently sent out for a delicious ice-cream party!

COME TO HELLO KITTY'S
SUPER SUNDAE CELEBRATION!
HERE'S THE SCOOP:
DAY: SUNDAY, FEBRUARY 1
TIME: 4 PM UNTIL 6 PM
WHERE: HELLO KITTY'S HOUSE
WEAR YOUR SUNDAE BEST!
R.S.V.P. TO 555-1212 BY JANUARY 25.

At the Super Sundae Celebration, Hello Kitty and her friends shared supertasty ideas for delicious ice-cream treats. Here's one of Hello Kitty's favorite recipes:

# Hello Kitty's Super Sundae

**What you need:**
* Vanilla ice cream
* Strawberry ice cream
* Chocolate syrup
* Whipped cream
* Rainbow sprinkles

**What you need to do:**

* Place a scoop of vanilla and a scoop of strawberry ice cream in a shallow dish.

* Pour chocolate syrup over the ice-cream scoops.

* Top with whipped cream.

* Add rainbow sprinkles.

## Thank-yous

Thank-you notes are important. When you receive a gift, Hello Kitty thinks it's best to send out a thank-you note within ten days. Here's a thank-you note she wrote to Tracy.

Dear Tracy,

Thanks so much for the adorable backpack. I will love wearing it to school. The apples on it are so cute. You are a great friend and always seem to choose gifts with real a-peel!

Thanks again for the gift. I'll enjoy using it.

Love,

Hello Kitty

*Thanks so much!*

## Thoughtful Thank-you Note Touches

Collect all of your special thank-you note supplies in a box. Put all your superspecial stationery stuff in one place. Your box can include:

* Pretty stationery and paper in different sizes, colors, and textures

* Personalized return address labels

* Fun postage stamps

* Colored pencils, glitter and metallic pens, crayons, and markers

* Edging scissors

* Fun stickers, like the ones in this book

* Glitter, sequins, and confetti

* Ribbon, lace, and sewing scraps

* Scissors and glue

## There's More Than One Way to Say Thank You!

**Jazz up an ordinary thank-you note by saying thank you in another language.**

Arabic: *dankie*

Cantonese: *doh jeh*

Finnish: *kittos*

French: *merci*

German: *danke*

Greek: *efharisto*

Hawaiian: *mahalo*

Hebrew: *toda*

Italian: *grazie*

Japanese: *arigato*

Portuguese: *oblig-ado*

Russian: *spasibo*

Spanish: *gracias*

Swahili: *asante*

Tagalog: *maraming salamat*

Yiddish: *a dank ach*

Zulu: *ngiyabonga*

ISBN S-TK9-68015-8

# Q&A

**HELLO KITTY SAYS:** "Hand-written notes make lasting impressions."

**Q:** Hello Kitty, I forgot to send a thank-you note for a gift I received. Is it too late to send one?

**A:** While it's best to send a thank-you note within ten days of receiving a gift, a note that is sent later will still be appreciated. A belated thank-you note should include the same ingredients as one that was sent on time: a thank-you to the giver and a mention of the specific gift, something special about the gift, a nice closing comment, and your name. Slide your note into an envelope, stick on a stamp, and send it. Suddenly, you're out of your sticky situation!

# Telephone and Internet

☀ Keep your calls short.

☀ Ask if it is a good time to talk.

☀ Don't call early in the morning (before 9 a.m.), late at night (after 9 p.m.), or at dinnertime (between 5 and 7 p.m.).

☀ Speak in a clear voice.

☀ Let the phone ring at least six times before hanging up.

☀ If you get an answering machine or voice mail, don't hang up. Leave a short message.

## Answering Machines

If an answering machine or voice mail takes your call, be sure to give your name, the time, and the reason for your call. Here's an example: "Hi. This is Hello Kitty. I'm calling Fifi about the fund-raiser at school. It's four in the afternoon. Fifi, would you call me back? My number is 555-1212. Thanks."

# Etiquette

### Taking a Message

When taking a message, ask the caller to repeat any information that's unclear. Say "Can you spell that, please?" if you're not sure about a name that is said. Read back all the telephone numbers to be sure you've gotten them right.

### Hello Kitty's Message for Mama

Mama, Mrs. Brown called today at noon. Her phone number is 555-1234. She would like you to call her back with your apple pie recipe.

### Ending a Call

To wrap up a phone call, say, "It's been great talking to you. I have to go now," or "I've got to say good-bye now. Someone else needs to use the phone."

### Sorry, Wrong Number

If you answer the phone and the caller has dialed a
wrong number, be polite about the mistake. Don't give
out your phone number. Instead ask, "What number did you dial?" If
the number the caller gives isn't your number, let them know. If it is,
say, "That's our number but there is no one here by that name."

## Ask Hello Kitty

**Q:** Hello Kitty, what do I do if I dial a wrong number?

**A:** If you call a wrong number, don't just hang up quickly. Simply
say, "I'm sorry. I think I have the wrong number. Is this 555-
1212?" It's as easy as that!

### Basic Netiquette: E-mail Manners

✻ Don't shout. The use of capital letters for emphasis is the
equivalent of shouting and is considered rude.

* Do give people enough time to respond.

* Don't assume your message has been received.
If you don't get a response, check to see that your
message was received before you assume the recipient is
inconsiderate.

* Do tell a parent if you come across troubling information on the
Internet.

* Don't get involved with chain letters.

* Do use your best spelling and grammar.

* Don't ever give out your address or telephone number without a
parent's permission.

* Do write positive things and avoid criticizing others or gossiping.

* Don't download attachments if you don't
know the source.

* Do limit the number of messages you send.

☀ Don't send a picture of yourself to someone you haven't met in person.

☀ Do remember that others may read your e-mail. Don't write anything you wouldn't want your friend's family members to read.

☀ Never use a parent's credit card number on the Internet without asking their permission.

☀ Don't write angry, mean, or threatening messages online.

☀ Do keep up face-to-face conversations with your friends. E-mail should never replace actual social get-togethers.

☀ Don't use e-mail as a substitute for messages that should be handwritten, such as thank-you notes.

☀ Don't pretend to be someone you're not when you're online.

☀ Do use emoticons (the little sideways faces you can create with letters and punctuation) to add an element of fun to your e-mails to friends. Here are some to try:

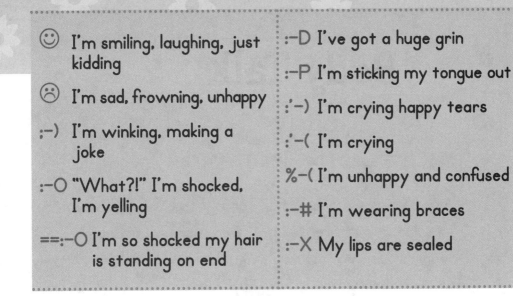

| | |
|---|---|
| ☺ I'm smiling, laughing, just kidding | :-D I've got a huge grin |
| ☹ I'm sad, frowning, unhappy | :-P I'm sticking my tongue out |
| ;-) I'm winking, making a joke | :'-) I'm crying happy tears |
| :-O "What?!" I'm shocked, I'm yelling | :'-( I'm crying |
| | %-( I'm unhappy and confused |
| ==:-O I'm so shocked my hair is standing on end | :-# I'm wearing braces |
| | :-X My lips are sealed |

## Shareware Solutions

If you share a computer with family members, here are some helpful hints:

* Do wash your hands before using the keyboard.

* Don't eat or drink near the computer.

* Do back up your files on disk.

* Don't tie up the phone line.

* Do use antivirus software to protect everyone's files.

# PART 10

# Body Talk

## Make a Lasting Impression

Your body language should convey to others that you're listening and interested in the conversation. You also want people to know that you're glad to see them. How can you do that through body language alone?

* Stand tall.

* Hold your head up.

* Look people in the eye.

* Dress appropriately.

* Be sure you are clean and neat.

body language

## Finishing Touches

As a fashion-forward girl, Hello Kitty knows how important good grooming is. She always chooses a private or semiprivate setting, like a bathroom or bedroom, for brushing and combing her hair and straightening her bow. Semiprivate settings like a public rest room or inside a car are also good locations for adding finishing touches. Applying a little bit of lip gloss or lip balm can be done at a table in a restaurant, but combing or brushing your hair should never be done near food.

## Ask Hello Kitty

**Q:** Hello Kitty, what should I do when I feel that I'm about to sneeze?

**A:** Cover your mouth and nose with a tissue before you sneeze. If you don't have a tissue, cover your nose and mouth with your hand. Then wash your hands after sneezing. If someone says "Bless you" or "Gesundheit," respond with "Thank you."

# Excuse Me!

*If you feel you need to burp,* do so as quietly as you can. Say "Excuse me" if you make a noise when you burp. If somebody else burps, say nothing.

*If you feel a yawn coming on,* cover your mouth. Don't comment about it. If someone you are with yawns several times, you may want to say, "I had no idea it was getting so late!" This gives the person a chance to make a graceful exit if she's tired.

*If you have the hiccups,* don't draw attention to yourself. If you want to use a tried-and-true technique that has always worked for ridding yourself of the hiccups (such as drinking water upside down from a glass or eating a spoonful of sugar), excuse yourself and do so in private. If someone you know has the hiccups, don't focus your attention on her.

# Special Events, Special Behavior

# PART 11

## A Family Affair

If you're attending a family event that celebrates a particular person (your aunt's birthday or your cousin's graduation), remember that she is meant to be the star of the day.

* Smile for the camera when it's time to pose for pictures.

* Show that you are excited to see your relatives.

* Join in activities.

* Remember that family events and traditions that may seem silly now will make for great memories.

## Wedding Belles

Girls can have roles at weddings as flower girls, bridesmaids, or guests. It's an honor to be asked to be in someone's wedding. No matter what part you're playing, you'll want your manners to be at their best.

If you've been chosen to be a flower girl or a junior bridesmaid, you will wear a pretty dress and share in the bride's special day. You will also be asked to attend a rehearsal.

*At the rehearsal,* you'll find out what you need to do during the wedding ceremony and reception. Listen carefully and ask any questions you may have at this time.

*During the wedding procession,* walk slowly and gracefully. Following the ceremony and prior to the reception, all of the members of the wedding party form a receiving line. Wedding guests will congratulate the bride and groom and introduce themselves to people they don't know. You can introduce yourself and explain how you are related to the bride or groom.

The reception usually includes food and music. At some point during the reception, the bride and groom will cut their wedding cake. When they are getting ready to leave the reception, the bride usually tosses her bouquet toward a group of unmarried women and girls. Jump for the bouquet, but don't push or shove anyone in an attempt to possess those petals!

## Good Cheer

How does Hello Kitty help cheer up those who are special to her when they are sick at home or recuperating at a hospital or care facility?

☀ First she finds out how the patient is feeling and whether or not a visit would be welcome.

☀ Then she asks the family and nursing staff what a good day and time would be for the visit.

☀ She keeps the visit short.

☀ She asks how the person is feeling but doesn't pose too many questions.

☀ She avoids making any negative comments about the person's appearance.

☀ She chooses a gift for the person such as a book, a video to watch, a magazine, or a small vase of flowers.

☀ She checks her watch and wraps up her visit after about twenty minutes.

# PART 13

# Being a Model Citizen

## National Niceties

How does Hello Kitty suggest you show your patriotism?

☀ Fly your country's flag.

☀ Celebrate your country's national holidays.

☀ Show respect during the national anthem.

☀ Let others know why your country is a great place to live.

☀ Read biographies about your country's heroes and heroines.

## Global Graciousness

Hello Kitty loves to explore the world. She always travels with a curious, friendly, and accepting attitude. Here is some of her best advice for people preparing to pack their bags for foreign travel:

☀ Learn the standard greeting and other common expressions in the language of the country you are visiting.

- Try the foods of the country. If they are eaten in a way that's different from what you're used to, show a willingness to try the new technique.

- Be aware that in some countries, loud laughter or conversation is considered offensive.

- Recognize that the people of some countries prefer punctuality. In other places, it is considered acceptable to arrive late.

- Avoid comparing the country you are visiting to your country.

- Show an appreciation for the customs, religions, language, and history of the country you are visiting.

## Be Polite to the Planet

Hello Kitty knows that being kind to the planet is just as important as being kind to her friends. She makes a point of recycling, throwing away litter, staying on hiking trails, and enjoying the great outdoors without leaving any evidence of having passed through.

## Show Your Hometown Hospitality

To show her hometown spirit, Hello Kitty's three favorite ways to give back to her community are learning about its history, attending local civic pride events, and volunteering.

With a little help from Hello Kitty, you've become an even more gracious and graceful girl. Practice excellent etiquette every day and make the world a more polite place!